# Helping at School

April Lee



INFOMAX COMMON CORE READERS

Rosen Classroom™

New York

Published in 2013 by The Rosen Publishing Group, Inc.
29 East 21st Street, New York, NY 10010



Book Design: Michael Harmon

Photo Credits: Cover ZouZou/Shutterstock.com; p. 5 Nagy-Bagoly Arpad/Shutterstock.com; p. 7 Anna Hoychuk/Shutterstock.com; p. 9 © iStockphoto.com/fullvalve; p. 11 © iStockphoto.com/Sadeugra; p. 13 © iStockphoto.com/esolla; p. 15 © iStockphoto.com/fatihhoca.

ISBN: 978-1-4488-8896-2
6-pack ISBN: 978-1-4488-8897-9

Manufactured in the United States of America

CPSIA Compliance Information: Batch #WS12RC: For further information contact Rosen Publishing, New York, New York at 1-800-237-9932.

Word Count: 26

# Contents

I carry the box.

I feed the mouse.

I close the door.

I clean the table.

I pick up the crayons.

I pick up the paper.

# Words to Know

crayon

mouse

paper

table

# Index